Caythorpe's History

By

Reg Baxter and Molly Burkett

First published by Barny Books,
All rights reserved
Memories recorded in 2006

No part of this publication may be reproduced or transmitted in any way or by any means, including electronic storage and retrieval, without prior permission of the publisher.

ISBN No: 1.903172.72.1

Publishers: Barny Books
              Hough on the Hill,
              Grantham,
              Lincolnshire
              NG32 2BB

              Tel: 01400 250246

Email: barnybooks@hotmail.co.uk

www.barnybooks.biz

My father worked on the railway. It was a six day week in those days and we used to walk down with him on a Saturday morning if we were up early enough. One of his jobs was to switch the points for the rails from the iron stone workings to connect with the main railway. He would leave his box at the side and tell us boys not to touch it.

"Yes Dad," we would say and as soon as he had gone off, we would look in it to see what he had. One day, we found a fog bomb and went off with it. We tried all sorts of ways to get it to go off but we couldn't get it to work so, in the end, we fixed it to the rail and went home.

passenger train in 1910

Perce Whaley from Hough on the Hill drove the locomotive for the iron stone workings and, as he was driving it towards the main line, there was a terrific explosion and Perce was out of the cab and running hell for leather towards the road. He thought it was a bomb. There was a lot of trouble about that.

You can see where the main railway line ran and where Caythorpe station stood. It is now the waste recycling factory. The old station-master's house is the offices.

The railway ran from Honington Junction to Lincoln and was part of the G.N.R. (the Great Northern Railway). It had been built by Kirkby and Parry of Sleaford and opened on the fifteenth of April, 1867.

The day before the grand opening, the Mayors from Newark, Lincoln, Grantham and Boston as well as other guests were taken over the new line.

The station and the road approaching it was decorated with bunting and evergreen for the grand opening. Even the goods shed had a special wooden floor laid for the occasion. It was one of the special days of the century for Caythorpe, so many guests in their fashionable clothes and smart coaches descended on the village.

The Chairman of the G.N.R. was George Hussey Parke and he lived at Caythore Hall. Caythorpe was his own, special station. He had a raised platform erected and had his own personal waiting room. He also had the right to stop and board any train that ran past the station.

There were nine return trains daily in the 1870s and one on Sunday. By 1914 there were two carriages on the train from Lincoln that would be attached to the main train at Grantham and travel to Kings Cross.

The stations were built some way from the village and Caythorpe's was no exception. The landowners had not wanted them running too close to their own homes. Many women who had gone into town for the shopping complained of the distance they had to walk with their heavy bags but that was later on.

Caythorpe Station about 1908

    The stationmaster was an important man and he wore a morning coat and top hat to show his position. Percy Biddle was the station master and his wife was disappointed when their son started to court a village girl. She thought that a son of a stationmaster should make a better match.

    The next station along the line was at Leadenham and, when the royal family were travelling to Scotland, the Royal train would be pulled into the sidings at Leadenham for the night. People from the villages would walk over the fields to the hill above Leadenham station hoping to catch a glimpse of Royalty.

    The railway was used for freight. Mail was sent by rail and so was the milk. Farmers would get their churns of milk to Caythorpe Station by half past six in the morning in time for the milk train but the freight that was mostly carried from Caythorpe was iron stone. In 1920 a siding had been built alongside the up platform for the stone traffic. Two trains a day carrying the iron stone would leave Caythorpe every day except Sunday taking the iron stone to the foundries at Scunthorpe.

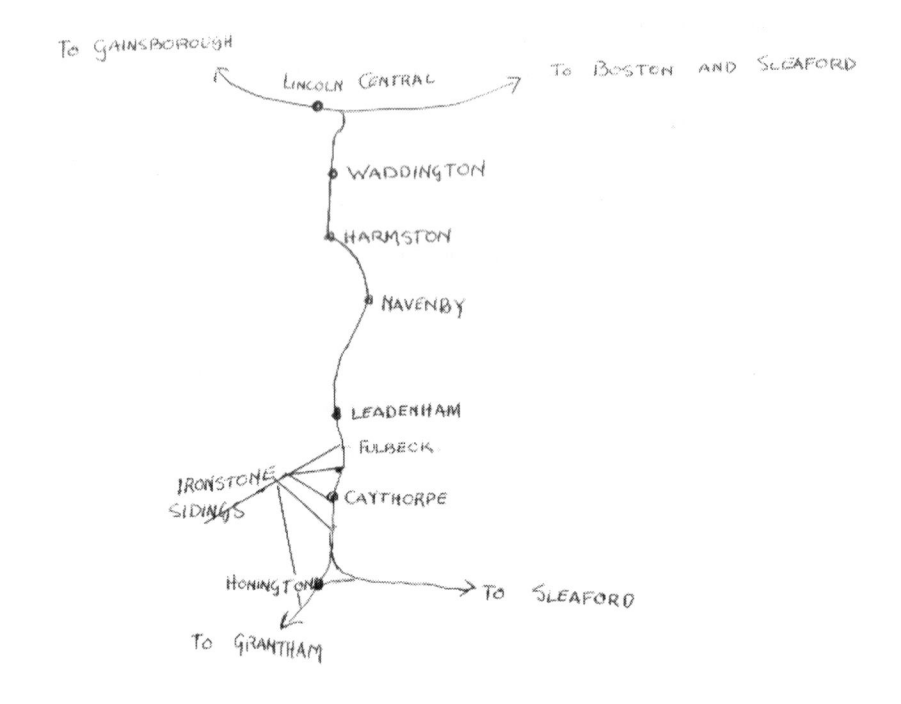

```
To GAINSBOROUGH
         ↖   LINCOLN CENTRAL   ↗ To BOSTON AND SLEAFORD
              •
              |
              • WADDINGTON
              |
              • HARMSTON
              |
              • NAVENBY
              |
              • LEADENHAM
              | FULBECK
IRONSTONE ⨯
SIDINGS    • CAYTHORPE
              |
    HONINGTON •————→ To SLEAFORD
         ↓
    To GRANTHAM
```

It was when they were building the railway, levelling the land between Caythorpe and Fulbeck that the iron stone seams became evident. Iron stone was extracted by The West Yorkshire Iron and Coal Company from 1870. They had leased land for this purpose from Caythorpe to the east of Fulbeck where the level crossing crossed South Heath Lane. By 1897, the seam had been worked out and work was started to the west of the station. The quarry south of Frieston was worked by W. Burke and Company and gradually spread along the Frieston - Hough on the Hill road. There was an extensive quarry system and lakes now stand where the iron stone was once worked. The lake, (the marshy area to the east of the Normanton Road) was drained in the 1980s.

"We used to ice skate there. The cadets from Cranwell used to come down there to skate as well. I was out on the ice one morning when I saw this aeroplane coming towards us and the pilot tried to come under the wires and he didn't make it. He crashed into the pylon and landed in the field just before the railway. It was one of those planes with double wings. We had time to get out of the way but it was a bit frightening. Miss Cragg, Percy Cragg's sister went and tended the pilot. The cadets thought it was a huge joke. No, the pilot wasn't badly hurt but the aeroplane was."

You can also see where the railway ran from the iron stone workings. In 1936, a tank engine named Munition was used to carry the iron stone. The bridge under which it ran is still there on the bend where the Hough road leaves Frieston. It then ran across the fields and along Love Lane to join up with the main Grantham line. Percy's brother, Lew, had a shed like a sentry box on the Carlton Road to stop any traffic when the locomotive was approaching. He didn't have a lot to do. There'd be people on bicycles and a few on horseback and there was the farm traffic which was mainly horse and carts before the Second World War. There were few cars on the road and those that there were belonged mainly to the gentry. The only person we knew who owned a car in the 1930s was the doctor, Doctor Dodson and he didn't always drive himself. He had a general handyman who would sometimes drive him. Then the schoolmaster, Mr Taylor, bought a car. He lived at Frieston. Miss Picker was the infants' teacher. She came from Welbourn on the bus. Our other teacher was Miss Baines from Fulbeck.

Caythorpe Station and Railway Bridge

There was a tarmac plant about a third of the way along the Hough road and they used the stone that the iron stone workings didn't want but it was closed down in the 1930s because one of the men fell into the vat and was killed.

The iron stone workings were the main employers in the time between the wars and men would walk miles to reach work each day and they started early.

"I used to leave home at six o'clock each morning to go to the bus stop in Frieston for the half past six bus and they would all be working when I passed the works and would often still be there when I came home at half past five."

A six-day working week was normal and an eleven-hour day was not unusual. A lot of the men had a bit of a smallholding to run when they did get home. Percy Whaley did.

You can still see where the iron stone seam ran parallel to Hough Road. Many of the footpaths that cross the area are the paths that the men used to get to the iron stone workings.

Caythorpe Station was closed to passenger traffic on the tenth of September 1962 and to all traffic on the first of November 1965.

Caythorpe was originally a Danish settlement. There were Roman settlements in the area and evidence of Iron Age homes have been found near Caythorpe. In the Domesday book, Caythorpe is listed under the land belonging to Robert de Vessey (Terra Roberti de Vecci)

'Aelfric had 19 caracutes and 2 bovates of land in lordship and 28 caracutes and 6 bovates of jusrisdiction taxable land and land for as many ploughs, that is 48.'

(A Caracute of land was approximately 120 acres.)

There were three hundreds (a measurement of land) attached to Caythorpe, those of Frieston, Normanton and Willoughby, now known as West Willoughby.

There were 113 freemen (who could rent land) with 32 ploughs, 50 villagers and 7 smallholders with 13 ploughs. Smallholders were able to rent smaller areas of land, enough to provide for their own needs. There were two churches and two priests, half a mill and 880 acres of meadowland

Three of Robert's men had jurisdiction (i.e. managed) over 12 caracutes and 7 bovates of this land and four and a half ploughs.

An Englishman had one curacute and five bovates and a plough.

The total value of this land before 1066 was £30 but was then revalued at £50.

Caythorpe was an important settlement and village land as far afield as Heckingtom came under its jurisdiction. A typical claim that was held at the time was brought by Gilbert of Ghent against Robert de Vessey, claiming that the meadow which was Aelfric's, his predecessor should rightly belong to him. The Wapentake stated that the same Aelfric had the whole meadow but did not have anything of it by right except by renting it for money.

Caythorpe High Street decorated for Queen Victoria's Golden Jubilee.

Mr Gilbert Hall is on the left beside Mr Champion and Mr Hughes. Mr Bayes is wearing the white hat and the boy with folded arms is the bakers apprentice.

By the end of the nineteenth century, there were three estates in the village, the owners of which owned most of the land. There was Holy Cross in the centre of the village. There had been a house on the site since the sixteenth century but it had been knocked down and rebuilt in the mid 1800s. It was taken over by the army in the Second World War. The estate was sold by Escritt and Barrell in 1946. The Baldwin family moved south. The house was demolished except for the stables which are now the village hall. The beech trees that stood behind the site of the garage on the Old Lincoln Road lined the drive to the house although they have now been felled but the two pillars which were at the entrance to the drive are still standing.

Arnhem Drive was once the gardens to Holy Cross and when people moved into some of the houses in the 1960s, they reported seeing a lady walking in their gardens at the same time every evening and taking exactly the same path, a path that went round the ornamental pond and the rose garden that had stood there for centuries. Some said it was the ghost of Lady Jane Grey (The Grey Lady) who was reputed to have stayed at Holy Cross before her marriage.

Old Ma Wilson lived at Old Frieston Hall – she used to collect the nursing money: 2s 6d a year. She was handy with her walking stick and would poke hard if you stood too near her.

Caythorpe Court stands on the ridge above the village and was owned by Lady Yarborough. This too was partly taken over by the army during the war and there is a commemoration plaque in the top yard remembering the men who fought at Arnhem and were billeted there. After the war, the estate was sold and Caythorpe became an Agriculture College until it amalgamated with Lincoln College of Agriculture at the turn of the century. Some of the land was divided and sold.

The College and buildings were then bought by PGL, a firm that develops holiday adventure and study centres for children between the ages of 7 and 16. The buildings have been completely modernised and the complex offers some of the most advanced equipment for children in Europe.

Caythorpe Court today

Activities offered at Caythorpe Court include kayaking, high ropes courses, climbing tower, zip wire, giant swing, abseiling, quad bikes, rifle shooting, fencing, archery, Jacob's ladder, trapeze, aeroball, football, raft building etc.

Caythorpe Hall stands in the land behind the Church. Two rooms in the house and the stable block were also taken over by the communications section of the Parachute Regiment during the Second World War while waiting to go to Arnhem.

Caythorpe Hall

Dick Appleton remembers, "We drew into Leadenham station at dawn and were marched to Caythorpe Hall and billeted over Lady Watson's stables. Beds had been prepared and we lay down to get some rest until Lieutenant Robertson (Golliwog Jam Robertson) appeared and told us that all meals were to be taken at Holy Cross. The village hall was the quarter-master's store and the top floor was the NAFFI.

Caythorpe was so different to our other wartime experiences. The people were so welcoming and the countryside so peaceful and beautiful. Those villages became endearing to me and I know that I am not the only soldier to feel that.

We settled down to P.E., runs, arms drill etc and we had to mount guard at Holy Cross. The guard house was adjacent to the two pillars at the end of the drive. M section had to march down to Holy Cross and, one day, the children snowballed us and one of the snow balls caught my rifle fore sight.

"There's water in your barrel," the orderly officer said and, when I tried to explain, I got the old routine, "Stop talking when you're speaking to an officer," followed by, "You shouldn't let the children snowball you anyway."

I got an extra guard duty for that.

The Passion Wagon used to go down to the town every evening but I was quite content with the Red Lion. There's been many a time when I've woken up on the grass patch in front of the doctor's house. (It is now a Home for the Elderly). Others found a similar resting place in the Churchyard.

Then it was D-day. The WAAFs packed the parachutes and when they asked, "Is it O.K. love?" we would say, "If it isn't we'll come back and change it."

D-day went and we were still at Caythorpe scouring the lanes for fair maidens.

Then it was the real thing and enough has already been said about Arnhem. It was a heart-rending moment when we were ordered to withdraw. We returned to Louvain, down the road to hell. We landed at Saltby Airfield and the tables were loaded with eggs and bacon etc. It was our first proper meal for a week. Then we were taken back to Caythorpe by lorry. It was free drinks all round that night. There was a long queue up the street at the post office as we all wanted to send telegrams home. There were so many empty billets, so many who hadn't made it back. Then it was home leave. I had my 21st birthday at home.

Working the land the old fashioned way with horses and plough

Sir Frank Watson was Chief Finance Adviser to the Egyptian government and lived in Cairo with his wife. They often used to visit Caythorpe and stayed with his wife's twin sister, Miss Reed who lived at Caythorpe Hall. All three of them rode with the Belvoir Hunt when the Walkers were visiting. The two ladies always rode sidesaddle, well the gentry did in those days. Miss Reed's horse fell jumping a hedge when they were following the hunt and she was killed.

We hardly ever went out of the village. There was everything that we needed here, not that we needed a lot. We grew our own vegetables and kept a pig in the sty. We ate well when we had a pig killed but always felt sad when we did. We always shared some of the fresh meat with our neighbours and they did the same when they killed their pig. I think that's the thing I miss most now, the togetherness and the readiness to help each other was always part of our lives in those days. We didn't have much but we were always prepared to share with people who were less fortunate than ourselves.

When Mrs Gibson was ill, we took it in turns to take her a lunch each day. When a new baby was born, somebody would fetch the bag and take it round to the new mother. This was an embroidered linen bag which contained well laundered baby clothes.

There were four hostelries in Caythorpe in the nineteenth century:

The Sun which was a Temperance Inn. It is now a private house in the High Street and has been renamed Hardwick House.

The Old Red Lion was an alehouse and people would collect the ale in jugs. Men from the iron stone workings would collect ale in buckets and jugs for the workers.

The new Red Lion and the Waggon are still public houses although the Waggon was smaller in size at the turn of the century and was part of a row of shops.

Polly Hewson with brother Bob Cragg –
landlord and lady of the Old Red Lion
(you can just see the pub sign near the top left hand window)

Delivery of beer in kegs to the Red Lion

The Red Lion today

The Eight Bells was a popular pub but the brewery shut it down in 1999 and it is now a private house.

Parson Sherriff with the beagles outside the Eight Bells

The Waggon was originally much smaller than it is today. There were three shops there with the entrance to the bar between the second and third shop. The cobblers and saddle maker was on the corner and Miss Edie Stevenett ran the shop next door. She sold everything from peppermints and elastic to buckets and hairpins. Her brother had the other room as his work shop. He was a photographer.

Mr Wilcox ran the bakery. There was nothing like the smell of the baking bread to make you feel hungry. The bakers was where the row of cottages are in the High Street along from the Waggon. There were big ovens at the back of the building. Miss Wilcox ran the post office in the building next door, the one that is end on to the High Street. Originally the post-office was opposite the Red Lion, the house where Mr and Mrs Goodban lived. He had been a Japanese Prisoner in the War. He became the head of Kings School in Grantham. When Mr Swithum took over the post office, he moved it to the present building, converting the kitchen to the post office.

Mr Green owned the butcher's shop situated opposite the Red Lion. There was a slaughterhouse at the back.

The Parish Church is dedicated to St Vincent who was martyred at Valencia in A.D.303 under the persecution of the Emperor Diocletian. It is not clear why a Christian martyr of the fourth century who lived and worked in the Saragossa area of Spain should be remembered in England but Archdeacon Brian Lucas, a former rector of Caythorpe, takes the view that as Vincent's refusal to deny Christ would have gone down well with the Knights Templar, the dedication might be due to the fact that the Order held the patronage when the Church was built.

Dr Fraser-Darling, the author of the second edition of the Church guide, thinks that it is likely that the building of the present magnificent Church is due to Lady Elisabeth de Burgh, a niece of Edward the second, who was very wealthy and owned the lordship of Caythorpe and Frieston. Building started early in the 14th century and was largely completed before the Black Death in 1348.

It is a double naved Church. A lofty and slender two and a half bay arcade divides the two naves east to west. The columns are octagonal and the arches double chambered. The North Aisle on the far side, was built by Gilbert Scott in about 1860 because the Church was not large enough to accommodate the congregation. Its architectural style is sadly out of keeping with the original building and destroys the symmetry of the original layout.

The Arnhem Window in the Church

On September 15th, 1974, the North Aisle was named the Arnhem Aisle and dedicated by the Bishop of Grantham to the memory of the men of the First Airborne Divisional Signals who were billeted in the Parish and neighbourhood before flying to Holland in their valiant attempt to establish a bridgehead over the River Rhine at Arnhem on September 17th 1944.

Arnhem Veterans marching through Caythorpe High Street on Arnhem Sunday. General Dean-Drummond is taking the salute.

This was the famous Market Garden. The friendship and fellowship between the villagers and soldiers has lasted to this day. The first Sunday in September is Arnhem Sunday when old comrades return to the village that cared for them in darker days. Major General Anthony Deane-Drummond in his book, "Return Ticket," writes warmly of the villagers' admiration and possessive pride in their local airborne unit. Arnhem Sunday is still celebrated throughout Lincolnshire. At the time, Major General Deane-Drummond was a Major, second in command of the Airborne Signals. He returns regularly to take the salute in Caythorpe High Street.

Today's paras provide a Guard of Honour for the veterans

The Parachute Signals Squadron and its Old Comrades Association have fostered this enduring relationship which is always supported by present members of 216 Signal Squadron (now a part of 16 Air Assault Brigade) when operational conditions allow. They presented a specially woven carpet incorporating the Badges of the Parachute Regiment and the Royal Signals which was laid in the North Aisle. In 1994, No 216 Parachute Signal Squadron donated the stained glass window in memory of Airborne Signallers, including the two soldiers who fell in the Falkland Islands War of 1992. Also on the wall of the Church are the memorials to those men from Caythorpe who were killed in the two world wars and one to the 13 Signallers serving with 1st Airborne Signals in North Africa, Sicily and Italy, 1942-5.

A Methodist Chapel stood in Chapel Lane. It is now a modern furnishing show room.

"We used to go to Church in the morning and the Chapel in the evening. Even the vicar used to come with us. Daisy Corby used to play the organ and she couldn't half bang

out the hymns. Everybody sang. Daisy had seven children and they all joined in the singing but then the congregation started to dwindle until there were only a few of us going."

The Great War 1914-18

R.S. Anderson	Albert Bates	Thomas Albert Bird
Alex Carr	Albert Charles	H. Cooper
Joseph Covell	Walter Crowley	H. Fisher
Thomas Green	Robert Handley	Joseph Hempsall
John Richard Lound	William Lound	Thomas Lound
A. Parr	Thomas Richmond	Jasper F. Royds
George Speed	Charles William Wandby	
G Wells	Walter Wetherill	David Wetherill

World War 2

Philip G. Clayton   Gerald L. Dodson   Albert Godson
William Edward Shillaher

Falkland War Royal Parachute Signals

Major M.I. Forge   Sgt J.J. Baker

Iraq War

LT. Philip Green   Patrick Marshall Sqdn. Ldr.

Men killed at Arnhem, billeted and commemorated in Caythorpe Church

Capt S L Batch	Lt R A Gregg	Sigm J E Bloomfield
Cpl P E Day	Sigm J Dean	Sigm G C Dunning
Sigm T Ellam	Driver A B M Frew	Sigm J D A Gault
Sigm R L W Harris	Driver R H Hibbit	Sigm H Middling
Sigm D J Norbury	Sigm L J Oxenham	Sigm J A L Peters
Sigm C E Smith	Sigm E Southward	Driver C D Spires
Sigm D W Stewart DCM	L/Cpt A W Thompson	Sigm A Thomson
L/Cpl J Watkins	L/Sgt L Westall	Sigm R C Wiles
Sigm D J V Wolfe		

Sigm = Signalman

Caythorpe Football Teams including Henry Lumley, Mr Dewey, Frank Pickering, Vernon Rimington, Carl Ansom, Derek Godson, Jim Baxter, Benny Clayton, Freddie Wakeland, Jack Dewey, Louis Rimington, Rum Rick.

"We bought our farm in Love Lane from Mr Baldwin who lived at Holy Cross in 1946. He had been a wool merchant in York and carried on his business when he moved to Caythorpe. The Baldwins employed a lot of people in the house and the family were well liked in the village. They had bought Holy Cross from Colonel Royds. He had moved out of the village when his son was killed in a motor bike accident on Wellingore Hill. He had one other son who was mentally retarded. He moved to Stubton Hall from Caythorpe and when he died he left the hall for the care and education for students with special needs."

The estate was sold by Escritt and Barrell in 1946. It was about that time that Mr Grey bought the Hall. We used to play football in one of his fields and he wanted the use of it back so we had to find somewhere else. Mr Charlesworth who lived at Frieston let us use the field where his cows grazed. He took them out on a Saturday afternoon and we had our football matches. It was a bit tricky missing the cow pats but we were generally a bit more skilful at it than the other side.

Boys Football Team
Including Edgar and Carl Anson,
Peter (Pop) Endley and David Jollands

Then General Welby Everard said that he would sell us the field for £1,000. We had all sorts of fund raising events to get the money and Colonel Briggs had a Community grant towards it. That is how the village got their playing field. We used to change in a corner of the field until some more money was raised to build the changing rooms. In 1999, the police force were looking for a site to build the police office in the village. They bought a piece of land from the playing field committee. It is the money from this sale that is funding the new pavilion along with a grant from the lottery.

Freddie Siddons, Don Patterson and Reg Baxter – entrants in the four legged race at the village fete.

    The village hall was originally the stables to Holy Cross and some people still claim that they can smell horses in there on a wet day. Dances had been held there during the war and a fund was started so that it became the village hall. A committee was set up. The trouble was that not many of the people named on the committee knew that they were on it. It was a very lively time in the village until Dr Pimlett took over. A proper committee was set up and a village fund organised. The trustees of the village hall are members of the Parish Council and the hall is managed by the Village Hall Committee.

Caythorpe is now a thriving, modern community with two pubs, a store, a post office and a fish and chip shop. Several new estates have been built and old cottages have been modernised. There is a Parish Council which is elected every two years, a village hall committee, a playing field committee, a May fete committee, a social club committee, there is a bowls club, the women's institute, play group, pre school group, mothers and toddlers club, brownies, badminton club and a craft club.

"Men who have served together have developed an affinity with the area from where we left to go to Arnhem. Caythorpe has and always will hold a unique and special place in our hearts"

Major Lewis Gooden, Arnhem veteran.

Caythorpe High Street

Church Lane with the village sweep, Gandy Codd is in the picture, he had difficulty in pronouncing his words but he could imitate birds. He was an expert with the call of a cuckoo.

Aerial view of Caythorpe